CARS

HUMMER

Michael Bradley

 Marshall Cavendish
Benchmark
New York

Marshall Cavendish Benchmark
99 White Plains Road
Tarrytown, NY 10591-5502
www.marshallcavendish.us

Library of Congress Cataloging-in-Publication Data

Bradley, Michael, 1962—
Hummer/ by Michael Bradley.
p. cm. — (Cars)
Includes bibliographical references and index.
ISBN 978-0-7614-2981-4
1. Hummer trucks—Juvenile literature. 2. Automobiles, Military—Juvenile
literature. I. Title. II. Series.
TL230.5.H86B73 2009
629.222'2—dc22
2007024633

Photo research by Connie Gardner

Cover photo by Ron Kimball/www.kimballstock.com

The photographs in this book are used by permission and through the courtesy of: *Corbis*: Najlah Feanny, title page, 9 (B); David Cooper/Toronto Star, 6; Jose Manuel Ribeiro/Reuters, 9 (T); Bettmann, 13; Alan Schein Photography, 16; David Rae Morris/epa, 18; Mihai Barbu, 19; Gene Bievins, 21, 22; Car Culture, 26, 27; *Ron Kimball/www.kimballstock.com*: back cover, 28, 29; *Alamy*: Mark Scheuern, 4; Guy Spangenberg, 20 (B); Robert Bukaty, 24; Claude Thibault, 25; *AP Photo*: 10, Mike Derer, 7; Richard Drew, 14; *Everett Collection*: Columbia, 8 ; *Getty Images*: Scott Nelson, 5; Timothy A. Clary, 15; Jeff T. Green, 20 (T); *The Image Works*: Roger Violett, 12.

Publisher: Michelle Bisson
Art Director: Anahid Hamparian
Series Designer: Daniel Roode

Printed in Malaysia
1 3 5 6 4 2

CONTENTS

This is the Hummer that was bought at an auction for $1.25 million. It features airbrushed murals depicting scenes from the war in Iraq.

CHAPTER ONE
A STAR IS BORN

There are some pretty expensive vehicles out there. Rolls-Royces. Bentleys. Maseratis. But none of them could come close to this one. In January 2007, at the Barrett-Jackson Auto Auction in Arizona, someone paid $1.25 million for the Hummer CNN reporters had used to cover the war in Iraq.

Hummers have been used extensively by the United States in Iraq and the Middle East. In 2003, U.S. soldiers drove their Hummer to the scene of a car bombing at the Jordanian Embassy.

The money went to help build houses near hospitals for families who had military **personnel** recovering there. It was a good cause—and one expensive car. It

Hummers are big! The gas-efficient Smart Car fits sideways into the space taken up by the bigger car's rear end.

had been completely fixed up, of course. People could see the change take place on The Learning Channel's *Overhaulin'* series. The idea that someone would spend that much money shows just how cool the Hummer is to people.

It was another part of the growing **legend** of the vehicle. It goes with the great stories of the Hummer's service in the military and its lightning-fast rise in **status** among American consumers. What was once a fully **functional** combat machine used to support the U.S. armed forces has been turned into a symbol of power and style on roads throughout the country. In less than two decades, Hummer has gone from the dusty world of combat to the shopping mall and soccer field. But it has never lost its muscular style or its standing as one of the coolest **sport-utility vehicles** (SUVs) around.

Sure, some weren't too happy with the Hummer. They disliked its poor gas mileage and its size. And they had a point. But in a country where bigger is seen as better, the Hummer had enough fans to survive and **thrive**. Today, there are three **versions** of the vehicle, including a smaller model that still offers the same rugged **personality** as its bigger brothers.

Hummer excitement appears to know no boundaries. There is even a Hummer cologne, for those who want to smell like the rugged outdoors.

Hummers can be small—though even a toy-sized Hummer H$_2$ is big enough for an adult-sized employee to ride in comfortably!

7

Hummers have appeared in lots of movies. Here, a Hummer crashes through a house in the 2003 movie *Bad Boys 2*.

In December 2006 Hummer introduced a version of the vehicle that makes its own oxygen. The concept car has **algae**—which produces breathable air for drivers—growing in the side panels. What's next, a Hummer that cleans itself? Hummers have appeared in video games. They have been in movies and on TV shows ranging from *Power Rangers* to *The Simpsons*. There is also a Hummer racing team that drives in off-road events.

U.S. team Robby Gordon and Darren Skilton drive their Hummer through Martinlongo, Portugal, in the second stage of the Lisbon-Dakar rally on January 1, 2006.

The Hummer's huge front grill is the first sign that this is one big car!

It seems like the Hummer is capable of just about anything. Each new model designed to provide greater use for the military seems to produce another set of new features for regular citizens. The Hummer's high ground clearance, sturdy frame, and powerful engine make it perfect for crossing rugged **terrain**. It also comes in handy in bad weather on suburban streets. That's what has made Hummer so popular. It has given drivers a sense of security they can't get from other vehicles.

When you see that distinctive Hummer front grill, you'll know that while Hummer continues to do its job on the front line, it cleans up nicely for the rest of us, too.

Female employees worked on the Jeep assembly line at the Willys-Overland plant in Toledo, Ohio, thoughout World War II.

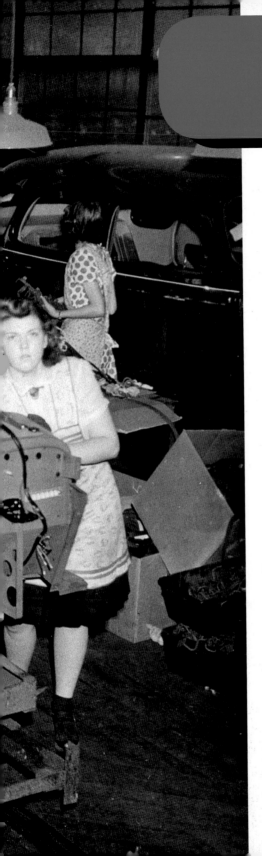

You may think the Hummer is a new concept, but it was actually more than fifty years in the making. That's right—way before Arnold Schwarzenegger and CNN were driving around in their Hummers, a big idea was being developed.

It started back in 1940, when a company called Willys-Overland created the first all-purpose, four-wheel-drive truck. They called it the GP, short for General Purpose, because it could go anywhere. Before long, the name was changed to Jeep. It was put to big use by the U.S. Army in World War II and became even more popular during the Korean War, when 150,000 Jeeps were built.

Over the next three decades, Jeep had several different owners. One was AM General, which in 1979 was given a chance to bid on the contract to build a new vehicle for the army. It would go anywhere and do almost anything and was called a High Mobility Multipurpose Wheeled Vehicle, or HMMWV (Humvee). It would be expected to move quickly over many different types of terrain. It would have to carry soldiers and heavy gear. It would need to support tanks in combat and climb steep hills. In other words, it needed to be the biggest, toughest truck out there.

Four years later, AM General had a contract to build 55,000 of these vehicles over a five-year period. Even though the company lost money on the first series it built, it had a truly **satisfied** customer because the army loved it. The Humvee went through water, rolled over rocks, and rarely broke down. By the end of the 1980s, the Humvee legend began to grow.

During the 1984 U.S. operation in Nicaragua, a helicopter dropped one of the vehicles into a combat situation—and into a thick patch of mud. No problem. A soldier cranked it up and drove it straight out of the **muck**. Another Humvee took a bullet

An M-998 Humvee drives along a road in the Kuwaiti desert during the 2003 Operation Iraqi Freedom. Oil wells set ablaze by retreating Iraqi forces burn in the background.

In 1983, AM General won the contract to create what would become the new official vehicle of the U.S. Army—the HMMWV, or Humvee. The letters stand for high mobility multipurpose wheeled vehicle.

Arnold Schwarzenegger drives a 2001 concept Hummer H$_2$ through Times Square for its New York City debut. Schwarzenegger was the first civilian to own a Hummer.

off its windshield, saving its driver. This was a great performance, and just the beginning. In 1990, fifty Humvees were used for ground **assaults** in Iraq, and they were unstoppable. The vehicles transported troops, dodged land mines, and launched missiles. Best of all, their work was shown to the whole world on news stations. This was a quick, strong machine that was better than a Jeep and could travel over just about anything.

No wonder Schwarzenegger wanted one. Long before he was governor of California, he was a movie star. When he was filming *Kindergarten Cop*, Schwarzenegger saw a Humvee drive by the set and figured it was perfect for a tough guy like him. So, in 1991, AM General made him a special Humvee. It was so cool that other people wanted one. In 1992 the company started making versions for the general public. **Demand** was slow at first, in part because the vehicle cost $100,000. But the Hummer, as many were now calling it, continued its military successes, and demand grew.

AM General knew how to make Hummers for battle, but it needed help getting them out on U.S. roads. It became a partner with General Motors, which created an SUV perfect for the daring, individualistic driver. First came the H_1. It was followed by the H_2 in 2002. Finally, in 2006, the H3 arrived. It was a little smaller than the others, but it hadn't lost that tough Hummer personality.

The 2007 Hummer H_3 on display at the New York International Auto Show. The H_3 is smaller than its older brothers but no less eye-catching.

The Hummer H₁—the first civilian Hummer—was every bit as powerful as the military Humvee.

Decades in the making, it was known as the world's most serious 4x4, and nobody could argue with that. When the first **civilian** Hummers rolled off the **production line** in 1992, buyers could be sure that while the SUV was ready for use on local roads, it stayed true to its original purpose.

Even though the inside looked a lot cleaner, and the exterior was more polished than its military cousin's, the Hummer's guts were army all the way. The **drive train**, body, frame, and **suspension** were identical to what was inside the Humvee. And that was the vehicle that made the trip from London to Beijing over the **grueling** roads of central Asia.

Humvees were deployed to New Orleans after Hurricane Katrina devastated the city.

As a result, drivers could travel in comfort. They knew they would be able to handle anything the elements could throw at them—often with greater ease than owners of other SUVs. If it was good enough for the rugged terrain and conditions of the world's toughest climates, it was good enough for Main Street, USA.

Those who wanted more proof of what the Hummer could handle could check out the arrangement set up between The Hummer Club Inc. and the American Red Cross. They worked together to form Hummer Owners Prepared for Emergencies (HOPE), a relief organization designed to use Hummers to provide help in disaster situations. HOPE helped out during the days following Hurricane Katrina, when so many people along the Gulf Coast needed help. So, the Hummer was rough and tough. But it also looked good.

The most **distinctive** feature of the H_1 was the grill. It looked like a toothy grin between two wide-eyed headlights. It was different than anything else on the road and gave the Hummer a personality like no other. Of course, there were some changes that had to be made. For instance, windows had to be added. Buyers wanted power locks, mirrors, and air conditioning. The Hummer may have started as a military vehicle, but it was supposed to be comfortable, too.

The Hummer is not something to buy when you're on a budget, but looking is free. This gold-plated Hummer H_2 was on display at a luxury goods exhibit in Romania, where the average income is about $12,000 per year. The average Hummer costs five times that.

Hummer-brand laptops are available through Hummer dealerships. They are marketed as the laptop version of the car: the toughest semi-rugged computers in existence.

Even with all of those upgrades, the first Hummer was a little tough to drive. So, in the late 1990s, a more driver-friendly version **debuted**. It was the H_2. It had everything you could find in any other SUV—with the individual Hummer touch. By the time the twenty-first century was well under way, H_2 owners could get top-flight stereos, **navigation** systems, and adjustable seats. They would be driving in the most luxurious SUV out there, and they could be driving it across a mountain if they wanted. That was the beauty of the H_2: the perfect blend of comfort and rugged Hummer power.

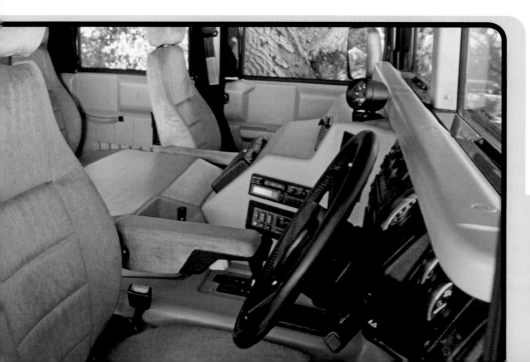

The interior of the Hummer is as luxurious and spacious as the exterior is tough.

Still, for some, the H2 was too big. So, in 2005, Hummer introduced the H3. It had the same concept as its big brothers, but it was a compact version. Its ground clearance was 7.5 inches (19 cm) lower, but the H3 had the same Hummer look, and it was designed for drivers who wanted the Hummer experience in a more

This fully modified H3 engine powered the car that NASCAR driver Robby Gordon drove in the 2006 Lisbon-Dakar rally. The car's chassis weighs 4,500 pounds (2,041 kg).

manageable form. It kept the powerful engine and the ability to climb and it could still handle the off-road demands. But the H3 was a less-expensive Hummer option that boasted better gas mileage and was easier to drive. It was the true next generation of the classic, but still a Hummer.

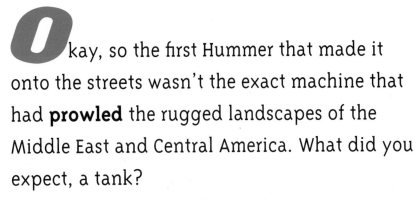

Okay, so the first Hummer that made it onto the streets wasn't the exact machine that had **prowled** the rugged landscapes of the Middle East and Central America. What did you expect, a tank?

Nope, the Hummer (H₁) had a civilian interior and windows that could roll up and down. But it also had some features that couldn't be found in the typical SUV. First, it was huge. The Hummer weighed just over 5 tons. It was also wider (about 86 inches wide) than the typical sport-utility model and could tow more than 9,000 pounds (4,091 kg). The Hummer also had all-terrain tires and a Central Tire Inflation

The Hummer H₃ may seem more compact than the first few models, but it can "survive the most punishing conditions that anyone could ever race," says NASCAR driver Robby Gordon.

23

HUMMER

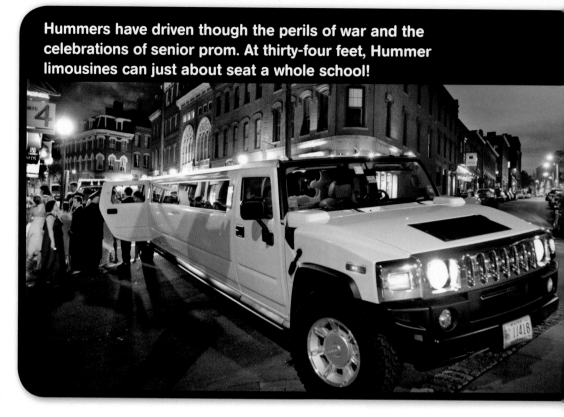

Hummers have driven though the perils of war and the celebrations of senior prom. At thirty-four feet, Hummer limousines can just about seat a whole school!

(CTI) system that allowed drivers to adjust the air pressure according to the ground the Hummer was covering. It boasted a 16-inch (40.6 cm) ground clearance and the ability to travel through 30 inches (76 cm) of water, although not at high speed. Its one-of-a-kind front end allowed it to go through deep ditches or over tall mounds of dirt without any front- or rear-end damage. And it could climb over a 22-inch (56 cm) wall without breaking down. No other SUV could come close to any of that.

The H_2 was a more **refined** animal, but that didn't mean it lost the trademark Hummer toughness. Though it looked more like a traditional SUV, it could drive through 20 inches (51 cm) of water without any problem. Its full-time four-wheel drive permitted the H_2 to tow

6,700 pounds (3,045.5 kg). And its strong chassis allowed the H2 to scale a 16-inch (40.6 cm) wall or step. Its **V-8 engine** could put out 320 **horsepower**, even more than the original Hummer.

It's possible to look at the H3 as the "little brother" in the Hummer family, but it's actually longer (by 2 inches) than the first Hummer. The ground clearance of 8.5 inches (21.6 cm) may not seem like much, but it is greater than all but a few sedans and on par with the majority of SUVs. Even if another SUV were to match the H3's clearance, it couldn't touch its toughness. The H3 can go through 24 inches (61 cm) of water at 5 miles per hour (8 kilometers per hour)—no small feat, given that standing water can ruin ordinary vehicles.

The H3 engine puts out 242 horsepower.

The Hummer is always developing in new ways. The H3 Open Top Concept car features a retractable cloth roof that lets in the sun, wind, and sky.

Like the H_2, it can get over a 16-inch (40.6 cm) wall with little difficulty. It may be smaller, but it's still wider than most of the competition. For instance, the H3 is nearly a foot (30.5 cm) wider than the Ford Explorer. Its five-cylinder engine can put out 242 horsepower—again, more than the Explorer. The H3 had it all, and because of its size and price (less than a quarter of the first Hummer's $140,000 price tag), it was far easier for a family to afford.

The 2007 Hummer H$_3$ can be outfitted for fire departments. Hummer offers a First Responder package that includes emergency lights, as well as a brushguard and off-road headlights for fire and rescue workers in heavily forested areas.

The Hummer family has something for everyone. What started with a movie star's desire to look tough has become an American sensation. Hummer has overcome obstacles and brought its rugged personality to the mall parking lot. It is quite a story.

And a great ride.

Vital Statistics

1992 Hummer H1

SPECIAL FACTS:
Grade: 60%
Side Slope: 40%
Fording: 30 inches (76 cm)
Tow Load: 9,303 lbs (4,229 kg)

Power: 300 hp
Engine Size: 403 ci/6.6L
Engine Type: Duramax turbo-charged diesel
Weight: 7,847 lbs (3,567 kg)
Top Speed: 90 mph (145 km/h)
0–60 mph (0–96.5 km/h): 16 sec

SPECIAL FACTS:
Grade: 60%
Side Slope: 40%
Fording: 24 inches (61 cm)
Tow Load: 4,500 lbs (2,045 kg)

2007 Hummer H3

Power: 242 hp
Engine Size: 226 ci/3.7L
Engine Type: Vortec 3700
Weight: 4,700 lbs (2,132 kg)
Top Speed: 98 mph (158 km/h)
0–60 mph (0–96.5 km/h): 8.9 sec

GLOSSARY

algae	A group of small organisms, sometimes found in water, which provide oxygen to their environment.
assault	An attack mission, generally quick and unexpected.
civilian	A person who is not in the armed forces.
debut	The first appearance of something in public.
demand	To ask for something forcefully.
distinctive	Standing out from others.
drive train	The part of an automobile that connects the transmission to the driving axle so power from the engine can make the wheels turn.
functional	Able to perform jobs.
grueling	Very difficult.
horsepower	A measure of the power generated by a motor or engine. The greater the horsepower (hp), the higher the speed at which an automobile is able to travel.
legend	A story handed down from generation to generation that usually has some of its roots in history.
manageable	Something that is easily handled.
muck	Thick, usually wet dirt that is hard to travel through.
navigation	The act of locating a place and then finding a way to travel there.
personality	The characteristics that make a person an individual.
personnel	Persons used in any kind of working situation, including an office or the military.
production line	A method of building a product that involves passing it from one station to another and adding a new part or performing a new task at each stop along the way.

prowl	To move along in a sneaky manner, as if in search of prey.
refined	Something that is very clean and precise.
satisfied	Content, or made happy by someone or something.
sport-utility vehicle (SUV)	A lightweight truck that can tow and carry cargo and also hold up to eight passengers.
status	The rank or position of a person within a group.
suspension	The system of springs and other supporting devices that are part of a vehicle's frame.
terrain	The qualities of a certain area of ground.
thrive	To be highly successful.
V-8 engine	A powerful engine that has eight cylinders to make a large vehicle move quickly.
version	One particular type of an item, such as a car model.

FURTHER INFORMATION

BOOKS

Edsall, Larry. *Hummer H3*. Saint Paul, MN: Motorbooks International, 2005.

Lamm, John. *Hummer H₂*. Saint Paul, MN: Motorbooks International, 2003.

Padgett, Marty. *Hummer: How a Little Truck Company Hit the Big Time, Thanks to Saddam, Schwarzenegger, and GM*. Saint Paul, MN: Motorbooks International, 2004.

WEB SITES

www.gmhummer.com

www.hummer.com

www.humvee.net

INDEX

Page numbers in **boldface** are photographs.

About the Author

MICHAEL BRADLEY is a writer and broadcaster who lives near Philadelphia. He has written for *Sports Illustrated for Kids*, *Hoop*, *Inside Stuff*, and *Slam* magazines and is a regular contributor to Comcast SportsNet in Philadelphia.